Land of Liberty

South Dakota

by **Thomas K. Adamson**

Consultant:
Mary B. Edelen
Director
South Dakota State
Historical Society

Capstone press
Mankato, Minnesota

Capstone Press
151 Good Counsel Drive • P.O. Box 669 • Mankato, Minnesota 56002
http://www.capstone-press.com

Library of Congress Cataloging-in-Publication Data
Adamson, Thomas K., 1970-
    South Dakota / by Thomas K. Adamson.
    p. cm.—(Land of liberty)
    Includes bibliographical references (p. 61) and index.
    Contents: About South Dakota—Land, climate, and wildlife—History
of South Dakota—Government and politics—Economy and resources—
People and culture—Recipe—Flag and seal—Almanac—Timeline.
    ISBN 0-7368-2198-8 (hardcover)
    1. South Dakota—Juvenile literature. [1. South Dakota.] I. Title. II. Series.
F651.3.A33 2004
978.3—dc21

                                                        2002156474

Summary: An introduction to the geography, history, government, politics, economy,
resources, people, and culture of South Dakota, including maps, charts, and a recipe.

Editorial Credits
Rebecca Glaser, editor; Jennifer Schonborn, series designer; Linda Clavel, book
    designer; Enoch Peterson, illustrator; Alta Schaffer, photo researcher; Eric
    Kudalis, product planning editor

Photo Credits
Cover images: Spearfish Canyon, Unicorn Stock Photos/Patti McConville; buffalo
on prairie in Custer State Park, Maxine Cass

AP Photo/Ted S. Warren, 50; Avera McKennan Hospital and University Health
Center, 38; Capstone Press/Gary Sundermeyer, 54; Corbis, 26; Corbis/AFP, 37,
41; Corbis/Bettman, 25, 28–29; Courtesy of University of South Dakota, 53;
Creatas, 57; Digital Vision, 1, 4; Houserstock/Dave G. Houser, 48–49; John Elk
III, 15, 42–43; Karen Foland, 31; Kent and Donna Dannen, 8, 32, 56; North
Wind Picture Archives, 21, 58; One Mile Up Inc., 55 (both); Rebecca Glaser, 16;
Stock Montage Inc., 18, 22; Tom Till, 12–13; Unicorn Stock Photos/Alice
Prescott, 44; U.S. Postal Service, 59; The Viesti Collection Inc./Joe Viesti, 63;
Visuals Unlimited/Tom Edwards, 17

Artistic Effects
Digital Vision, Linda Clavel, PhotoDisc Inc.

1 2 3 4 5 6 08 07 06 05 04 03

Table of Contents

The faces of George Washington, Thomas Jefferson, Theodore Roosevelt, and Abraham Lincoln look out from Mount Rushmore.

Chapter 1

About South Dakota

In 1927, a puff of smoke appeared on the side of the mountain. A loud boom followed. Rocks tumbled down a hillside. Workers blasted at the granite mountain with dynamite. Over three years, the face of an American hero slowly took shape. Completed in 1930, George Washington's face was the first one carved into Mount Rushmore.

Mount Rushmore is one of the largest sculptures in the world. It features the faces of four American presidents. Each president's head is about 60 feet (18 meters) tall. Gutzon Borglum designed this huge sculpture. It took 400 workers 14 years to carve the faces into the mountain.

"My lands are where my dead lie buried."

–Crazy Horse, Lakota leader

The Crazy Horse Memorial in the Black Hills is the largest sculpture in the world, even though only the face is finished. Korczak Ziolkowski designed the Crazy Horse Memorial. In 1939, Chief Henry Standing Bear invited Ziolkowski to create a memorial to Indians. The memorial honors Crazy Horse, a Lakota leader who led his warriors to victory in the Battle of Little Bighorn. When the sculpture is finished, it will measure 563 feet (172 meters) tall and 641 feet (195 meters) long.

The Mount Rushmore State

South Dakota's nickname is the Mount Rushmore State. The state slogan is "Great Faces. Great Places." Mount Rushmore draws nearly 2 million people every year.

South Dakota is a Midwestern state. North Dakota forms its northern border. Montana and Wyoming lie to the west, and Nebraska is to the south. Iowa and Minnesota form the state's eastern border.

South Dakota Cities

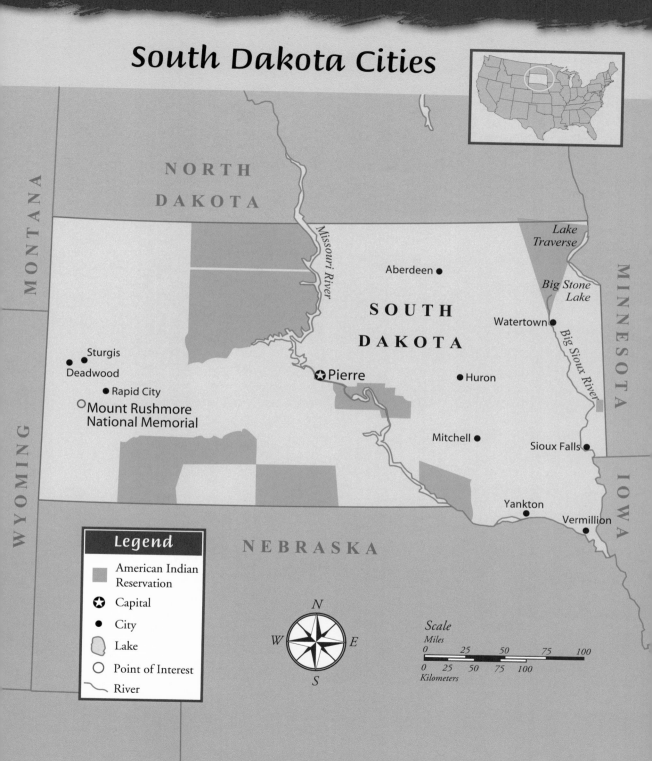

MONTANA

WYOMING

NORTH DAKOTA

SOUTH DAKOTA

MINNESOTA

IOWA

NEBRASKA

Missouri River

Lake Traverse

Big Stone Lake

Big Sioux River

Aberdeen

Watertown

• Sturgis
Deadwood

• Rapid City

○ Mount Rushmore
National Memorial

✪ Pierre

• Huron

Mitchell •

Sioux Falls •

Yankton •

Vermillion •

Legend
- American Indian Reservation
- ✪ Capital
- • City
- Lake
- ○ Point of Interest
- River

N
W E
S

Scale
Miles
0   25   50   75   100

0   25   50   75   100
Kilometers

The Missouri River runs through the Karl E. Mundt National Wildlife Refuge. The refuge protects bald eagle habitats.

Chapter 2

Land, Climate, and Wildlife

The Missouri River cuts through South Dakota and divides it nearly in half. People call the two halves of the state "East River" and "West River." When people drive across the state, they notice a big difference in scenery after crossing the river. Rolling hills and farmland cover the land east of the river. The western half of the state has prairies, ridges, and valleys. Mountains lie in the far west.

Geographers divide the state into three regions. The Central Lowlands lies in the east. The Great Plains lies in the west. The Black Hills is a low mountain range in the far western part of the state.

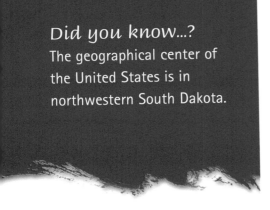

Central Lowlands

Eastern South Dakota is part of the North American Central Lowlands. It stretches from the Great Plains in the west to the Appalachian Mountains in the east.

Thousands of years ago, glaciers carved lakes in South Dakota's lowlands region. The glaciers also left behind low, rolling hills and rich soil called till.

Another feature of the Central Lowlands is the James River Basin. The James River flows from North Dakota to the Missouri River on the Nebraska border. It winds through the middle of the basin. The James River Basin is wide and flat. It is lower than the surrounding land.

Great Plains

The Great Plains covers most of western South Dakota. Rugged ridges and valleys lie west of the Missouri River. Steep, flat-topped mountains called buttes mark the western part of this region. Some buttes stand more than 400 feet (122 meters) above the surrounding landscape.

South Dakota's Land Features

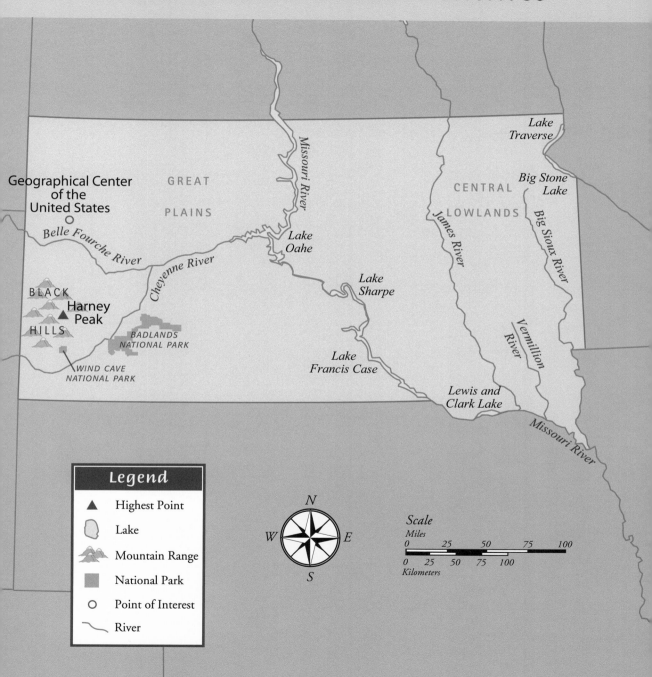

Geographical Center
of the
United States

GREAT

PLAINS

Belle Fourche River

Missouri River

Lake Traverse

CENTRAL

LOWLANDS

Big Stone Lake

James River

Big Sioux River

Lake Oahe

Cheyenne River

Lake Sharpe

BLACK

Harney Peak

HILLS

BADLANDS NATIONAL PARK

Vermillion River

WIND CAVE NATIONAL PARK

Lake Francis Case

Lewis and Clark Lake

Missouri River

Legend

▲ Highest Point

Lake

Mountain Range

National Park

○ Point of Interest

River

N
W   E
S

Scale
Miles
0   25   50   75   100
0   25   50   75   100
Kilometers

Areas of deep, narrow valleys and rocky hills, or badlands, are common in this area. Water wears away soft rock and creates deep cracks and valleys. Few plants grow in the badlands.

Black Hills

The Black Hills is a range of low and rugged mountains with deep canyons. It lies in western South Dakota. The pine trees that cover the mountains look black when seen from a distance. The state's highest point, Harney Peak, is

in this region. It is 7,242 feet (2,207 meters) tall.

The Black Hills is a popular vacation spot. The area's natural beauty provides opportunities for hiking and sightseeing. Mount Rushmore and the Crazy Horse Memorial are in the Black Hills. Limestone caves have formed under the Black Hills. People can tour Wind Cave, Jewel Cave, and Rushmore Cave.

A sunset makes the badlands
near Cedar Pass look red.

"We hold on to hopes for next year every year in western Dakota: hoping that droughts will end; hoping that our crops won't be hailed out . . . hoping that it won't be too windy on the day we harvest . . . hoping . . . Sometimes survival is the only blessing that the terrifying angel of the Plains bestows."
—Kathleen Norris, author of Dakota and resident of Lemmon

Lakes

South Dakota's largest lake is Lake Oahe. This long lake was formed when the Oahe dam was built on the Missouri River. Water collected behind the dam to form the lake. The lake is 250 miles (402 kilometers) long.

Three other dams were built on the Missouri River. These dams provide electricity and irrigation for farmland. They also form lakes. They are Lewis and Clark Lake, Lake Francis Case, and Lake Sharpe.

Climate

South Dakota has wide ranges in temperature. Cold winter temperatures differ across the state. In January, the northeast averages 10 degrees Fahrenheit (minus 12 degrees Celsius). The southwest averages 22 degrees Fahrenheit (minus 6 degrees Celsius). Brisk winds make temperatures feel even colder.

The Oahe dam provides electricity for five states.

Summers can be hot and humid. In summer, temperatures above 100 degrees Fahrenheit (38 degrees Celsius) are common. The Black Hills is usually cooler than lower areas in the state.

The western area of the state is drier than the eastern part. The western region receives about 13 inches (33 centimeters) of precipitation per year. The eastern region gets about 25 inches (64 centimeters) per year.

Falls Park

The largest city in South Dakota, Sioux Falls, is located on the Big Sioux River. The city grew near the waterfall called the Sioux Falls. Today, visitors view the falls from a five-story tower. People enjoy biking and hiking trails at Falls Park.

Wildlife

Millions of American buffalo once roamed the Great Plains. They provided food, clothing, and shelter for native peoples. When European settlers came to the Great Plains, they killed most of the buffalo. They sold the hides to people on the East Coast and in Europe.

People have tried to keep the buffalo from dying out. About 8,000 buffalo live in the state. South Dakota has more buffalo than any other state. A herd of 1,500 buffalo roams freely in Custer State Park. Other herds live on American Indian reservations and on private property.

Various other large mammals live in South Dakota. White-tailed deer live throughout the state. Many of them can be found roaming the Black Hills. Also living in the Black Hills are bighorn sheep, elk, and Rocky Mountain goats.

The ring-necked pheasant, the state bird, is found throughout the state. The ring-necked pheasant originally came from central Asia. About 2,000 years ago, people brought the birds to Europe. In the late 1800s, settlers brought them to North America. The pheasant population grew rapidly, and it continues to be a popular game bird.

A white ring around the male's neck gives the ring-necked pheasant its name.

American Indians living on the Great Plains hunted buffalo on horseback.

Chapter 3

History of South Dakota

Many groups of American Indians lived in present-day South Dakota when European explorers first came to the Great Plains. The Arikara lived on the northern Great Plains. They traded with the Mandan, Crow, Cheyenne, and Pawnee.

The Lakota, Nakota, and Dakota Indians lived to the east of the Arikara. They gradually moved west and later became known as the Sioux. The Sioux hunted buffalo and followed the herds on the Great Plains.

European Explorers

The first Europeans to explore what is now South Dakota were Louis-Joseph and Francois La Verendrye in 1743.

These French-Canadian brothers were looking for a water route that connected the Atlantic and Pacific Oceans. No such waterway existed.

French and Spanish fur trappers began moving to the area in the late 1700s. They hunted beavers. Trappers sold the fur to companies in Europe to make hats and other clothing.

Exploration and Fur Trade

In 1803, Thomas Jefferson purchased the Louisiana Territory from France. The United States paid $15 million for this huge territory. South Dakota was part of the Louisiana Purchase.

Jefferson asked Meriwether Lewis and William Clark to explore the land. They and a group of about 30 men left from St. Louis, Missouri, in 1804. The group followed the Missouri River. They met Sioux and Arikara Indians in South Dakota.

The fur trade grew throughout the 1800s. White settlers hunted buffalo and sold the fur. The Indians feared the settlers would kill all of the buffalo.

On their journey up the Missouri River, Lewis and Clark met American Indians.

Dakota Territory

In 1858, a soldier named John Todd made an agreement with the Yanktonai Sioux. He bought land in what is now southeastern South Dakota from the Sioux. He resold the land to American settlers. He and other settlers founded the town of Yankton. Soon, other towns were built in the area.

By 1861, enough settlers lived in the area to form a territory. Dakota Territory included North and South Dakota, and much of Montana and Wyoming.

The Homestead Act of 1862 promised free land to settlers. As settlers poured into the area, the Sioux began to fear they would lose their land. They attacked some of the settlers. The U.S. government built army posts to protect the settlers.

Chief Red Cloud organized many attacks against settlers to defend Sioux land.

Red Cloud's War

In 1863, the Bozeman Trail opened in Dakota Territory. Settlers used it to travel west. The trail crossed Sioux lands.

A Sioux leader named Red Cloud led attacks on settlers using the trail. These attacks became known as Red Cloud's War. The government sent army troops to defend the trail. The Sioux and Cheyenne defeated the soldiers.

In 1868, the government and the Sioux signed the Fort Laramie Treaty. This agreement ended Red Cloud's War and closed the Bozeman Trail.

The Fight over the Black Hills

The Fort Laramie Treaty also created the Great Sioux Reservation. This area covered land west of the Missouri River and included the Black Hills. The Sioux called the Black Hills Paha Sapa. This area was, and still is, sacred to the Sioux.

In 1874, General George Custer led a group into the Black Hills. Custer wanted to explore and find a place to build an army fort. Custer's group had about 1,000 people. Two miners, a photographer, four reporters, a band, and about 100 Indian scouts were among them.

Custer's group reported finding gold in the Black Hills. Newspapers spread the reports. The promise of gold in the Black Hills brought many people.

Under the Fort Laramie Treaty, the U.S. government was supposed to keep settlers out of the Black Hills. The army did stop hundreds of people in late 1874. But reports about the Black Hills area continued to appear in newspapers. Some people got past the soldiers and began searching for gold. After negotiations to buy the Black Hills failed, the army no longer stopped people from entering the Black Hills.

The gold rush forced the Sioux to fight for their land. Led by Crazy Horse and Sitting Bull, the Sioux repeatedly attacked the settlers. The U.S. military tried to stop the attacks. In 1876, the Sioux surprised General Custer and his men in present-day Montana. Custer and more than 200 of his men were killed in the Battle of Little Bighorn. It was the last major victory for the Sioux in the Dakota Territory.

After more fighting over the Black Hills, the Sioux Treaty was signed in 1877. This treaty gave the Black Hills to the United States. It also promised food and supplies for the Sioux. Many of the Sioux moved to reservations east of the Black Hills.

Wild Bill Hickok

Wild Bill Hickok was a famous Wild West man. He was a lawman, adventurer, and card player. People said he got out of control if someone made him angry.

Hickok spent time gambling in Deadwood, South Dakota. This mining town grew quickly during the 1876 Black Hills gold rush. Deadwood earned a reputation for its violence, gambling, and lawlessness.

Wild Bill Hickok was murdered in Deadwood. He was shot in the back while playing poker. He was holding a pair of aces and a pair of eights. These cards are still called the "dead man's hand."

Statehood

The capital of Dakota Territory was in Yankton until 1883. That year, Governor Nehemiah Ordway moved the capital to Bismarck. This city was in the northern part of the territory. People in the south began to think about statehood. When Benjamin Harrison became president, he signed the Omnibus Statehood Bill. This bill created North and South Dakota on

November 2, 1889. Harrison shuffled the papers so no one would know which one he signed first. The two states are usually listed alphabetically. North Dakota is the 39th state, and South Dakota is the 40th state.

Sioux Defeat

By 1890, the Sioux were starving. The U.S. government did not give them food and supplies as promised. Because of overhunting by white settlers, buffalo were scarce.

Most of Big Foot's band of Sioux, shown here near the Cheyenne River in 1890, were killed during the Wounded Knee Massacre.

Despite their bad conditions, some Sioux found hope in a new religious movement called the Ghost Dance. They believed the Ghost Dance would bring back the buffalo and their dead ancestors and restore their homeland. White settlers living near the Sioux reservations thought the Ghost Dance was a war dance. The U.S. government told the Indians to stop performing the Ghost Dance.

In December 1890, soldiers captured hundreds of Sioux. They took them to a village called Wounded Knee. No one knows who fired the first shot, but several shots were fired. In response to the first shots, the soldiers shot at the Sioux. Hundreds of Sioux men, women, and children were killed in the Wounded Knee Massacre. This massacre was the last armed battle between the U.S. military and the Sioux.

An Expanding Economy

In the early 1900s, South Dakota's economy depended too much on farming. Senator Peter Norbeck wanted to attract tourists to the state. He proposed establishing Custer State Park in the Black Hills. He received government money to build roads so tourists could travel there more easily.

The state government also brought in thousands of ring-necked pheasants to draw hunters to the state. The first pheasant hunting season in South Dakota was in 1919.

Great Depression and World War II

In the 1930s, the country suffered through the Great Depression (1929–1939). People lost jobs. Hot, dry weather caused droughts that killed crops. Strong winds blew the topsoil away, creating dust storms that swept across the plains. The dust drifted like snow.

As the droughts of the 1930s ended, the United States entered World War II (1939–1945). South Dakota farmers produced food for the war effort. Three air force bases opened in the state early in the war. The bases brought jobs to the state and helped South Dakota recover from the depression.

American Indian Issues

In 1973, several American Indians took over the village of Wounded Knee, South Dakota. These Sioux Indians joined members of a group called the American Indian Movement (AIM).

Armed American Indians escort a car out of Wounded Knee village in 1973. Members of the American Indian Movement occupied the village for more than two months.

They were protesting unfair treatment from the government. FBI agents tried to get the group to give up. AIM occupied the village for 71 days. A few gun battles broke out and two Indians were killed. Outnumbered and outgunned, AIM eventually gave up. But the protest made people aware of the Indians' concerns about civil rights.

In 1980, the U.S. Supreme Court heard a case about the Black Hills. The court ruled that the U.S. government had broken the Fort Laramie Treaty. The U.S. government paid the Sioux $106 million for the Black Hills. The Sioux refused to take the money. In a trust fund earning interest, it is now worth more than $500 million. The Sioux still refuse the money. They believe that land cannot be bought and sold.

In 1990, Governor George Mickelson declared a Year of Reconciliation between Indians and non-Indians. He hoped it would help people from different cultures understand one another. As a result, South Dakota changed its Columbus Day holiday to Native American Day.

Connecting the Schools

In 1996, Governor Bill Janklow began a program to bring technology to South Dakota schools. The state provided wiring, equipment, and training to schools. Now all schools in the state have Internet access. The Dakota Digital Network allows students to take classes from teachers across the state.

Even country schools in South Dakota have computers and Internet access because of a state program providing money for technology.

South Dakota's capitol building in Pierre was finished in 1910.

Chapter 4

Government and Politics

After statehood in 1889, South Dakotans argued about the location of the capital. A temporary capital was set up in Pierre. This town was in the middle of the state. People in Watertown, Huron, and Mitchell tried to make their cities the capital. None of the attempts were successful. In 1904, the legislature made Pierre the permanent capital.

State Government

Like the U.S. government, South Dakota's government has three branches. The executive branch carries out the state's laws. As the head of this branch, the governor serves terms of four years. The governor may not serve more than two terms in a row.

For example, Bill Janklow served two terms, from 1979 to 1987. He then ran again in 1994. He served two more terms, from 1995 to 2003.

Like most states, South Dakota's legislative branch is made up of two houses. They are the house of representatives and the senate. The state has 35 districts. Voters in each district elect one senator and two representatives. They serve terms of two years. They may not serve more than four terms in a row.

The court system in South Dakota is called the Unified Judicial System. The supreme court is the highest court. The governor appoints five justices to the supreme court. The justices serve for three years. Then citizens vote to either keep or reject the justices. Justices then serve eight-year terms. Circuit courts hear criminal and civil cases. Magistrate courts handle cases about less serious crimes.

Initiative and Referendum

South Dakota was the first state to have a system of initiative and referendum. The state adopted this system in 1898. With this system, South Dakota voters have some direct control in making state laws. Anyone may propose a new law using initiative. Five percent of voters from the last election for

South Dakota's State Government

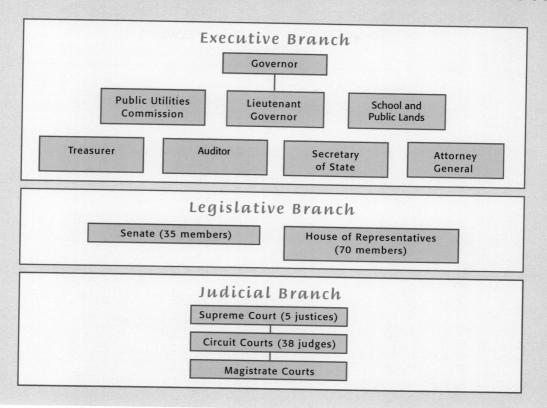

Executive Branch

Governor

Public Utilities Commission | Lieutenant Governor | School and Public Lands

Treasurer | Auditor | Secretary of State | Attorney General

Legislative Branch

Senate (35 members) | House of Representatives (70 members)

Judicial Branch

Supreme Court (5 justices)

Circuit Courts (38 judges)

Magistrate Courts

governor must sign a petition. If enough signatures are gathered, the proposed law goes onto a statewide ballot. Citizens then vote on that initiative.

Referendum gives voters a chance to accept or reject a law. When the legislature passes a law, South Dakotans can refer the law to a ballot. If enough signatures are collected on a

petition, the law can be put on a statewide ballot. Voters then choose whether to accept or reject a law.

Politics

South Dakota is generally a Republican state. Voters usually elect a Republican governor. The Republican Party has a large majority in the state legislature. South Dakota usually supports the Republican candidate for president. Despite this Republican support, South Dakota had two Democrats serving as the state's U.S. senators in 2002.

Tribal Governments

South Dakota has nine Sioux reservations. A tribal council governs each reservation. Each reservation also has its own court system. The South Dakota Office of Tribal Government Relations was established in 1949. This office helps the state government work with the tribal governments. They work together to solve problems the Sioux tribes may have.

Tom Daschle

Tom Daschle was born in Aberdeen, South Dakota, in 1947. He was the first in his family to graduate from college. After serving as an intelligence officer in the air force, Daschle entered politics. He started as an aide to South Dakota Senator James Abourezk.

Daschle was first elected to the U.S. House of Representatives in 1978. He was only 31 years old. He served four terms, then ran for U.S. Senate in 1986. He quickly gained the respect of his fellow senators as a hardworking leader.

In 2001, Daschle became the Senate majority leader. The highest ranking senator from the majority party holds this position. In 2002, he became minority leader when the Democrats lost control of the Senate. The minority leader has less power and influence. As minority leader, Daschle is still the leader of the Democratic Party in the Senate.

Daschle travels to each of South Dakota's 66 counties every year. He meets South Dakotans and listens to their concerns.

Sioux Falls is a regional center for health care. Avera McKennan Hospital provides many medical services.

Economy and Resources

South Dakota is not just a farming state. Several industries make up its economy. Computer production has become the state's leading manufacturing industry. Sioux Falls is an important financial and health care center. The federal government employs many people. They work on Indian reservations, Ellsworth Air Force base, and national parks.

Service Industries

Service industries make the most money for South Dakota. Business services, tourism, government, and trade are examples of service industries in the state. Trade includes the selling of groceries and farm products. Retail stores and

restaurants are also part of South Dakota's trade industry.

Financial companies are a large service industry in South Dakota. In Sioux Falls, 9,000 to 12,000 people work in the financial services industry. Citibank and Sears Payment Systems are two of the state's major credit card companies. Citibank employs about 3,200 South Dakotans. Financial companies pay taxes to the state and employ many people in Sioux Falls. South Dakota is a good place for financial and credit card companies to make money. The state places no limits on the interest rates they can charge.

The state's tourism industry is mostly centered in the Black Hills. People from all over the country go there to see the beautiful scenery. People visit natural caves and hike many trails in the mountains. They also camp, hunt, and fish.

Manufacturing

South Dakota has become a major producer of electronic and computer parts. Computer company Gateway is headquartered

Boxes with Gateway's signature cow design come off a conveyor belt at a South Dakota plant.

in North Sioux City. The company is known for packaging its computers in boxes with a Holstein cow design.

Several South Dakota companies also process food products. Sioux Falls, Mitchell, and Rapid City have meatpacking plants. Poultry products are processed in Watertown. Dairy products are processed in Aberdeen.

Agriculture and Mining

Farming continues to be an important industry in South Dakota. Corn is the state's largest crop. Wheat and soybeans are other major crops. Corn and soybeans are grown mostly in the southeastern part of the state. Spring wheat is grown in the north. Winter wheat grows in the southwest. South Dakota is the country's second largest producer of sunflower seeds.

Pastures cover about half the state. South Dakota ranchers raise cattle, hogs, and sheep. Sheep are raised in the west. Cattle and hogs are raised throughout the state.

Fertile soil is South Dakota's most important natural resource. Glacial deposits in East River created rich soil that is good for growing corn and wheat. Soil in West River is better for grazing cattle and livestock.

Most of South Dakota's mines are located in the western part of the state. Workers mine lignite coal and gold. The Homestake Mine in Lead (LEED), South Dakota, was once the largest gold mine in the western hemisphere. The Homestake Mine closed in 2001. It became too expensive to dig out the remaining gold.

Hay bales are a common sight on South Dakota farmland.

A Dakota dancer performs at the Fort Sisseton spring festival.

Chapter 6

People and Culture

South Dakota is where the Midwest ends and the west begins. It has wide-open spaces and a relatively low population. West River culture is more like the west, while East River culture is more like the Midwest. Lakota Indian culture is prominent on reservations and throughout the rest of the state.

People

European Americans in South Dakota are mostly descended from Norwegian, German, Irish, Czech, and English settlers. Most of these European immigrants arrived in the 1800s.

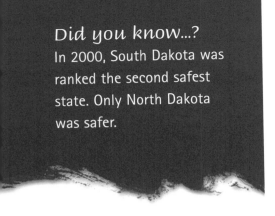
Some took advantage of the rich farmland. Some looked for gold in the Black Hills.

The nine Indian tribes in South Dakota are all part of the Great Sioux Nation. Indian reservations cover much of the state. American Indians make up more than 8 percent of the state's population.

The population in South Dakota is growing rapidly in the state's two largest cities. Rapid City, Sioux Falls, and the communities near them grew rapidly in the 1990s. But the small towns in the middle of the state have seen populations decline. More people are choosing to live and work in cities rather than work on farms.

Unique Attractions

South Dakota offers more attractions than just Mount Rushmore and the Black Hills. Unique attractions reflect the variety of the state's character. Wall Drug, the Sturgis Motorcycle Rally, and the Corn Palace are three of the most famous.

South Dakota's Ethnic Backgrounds

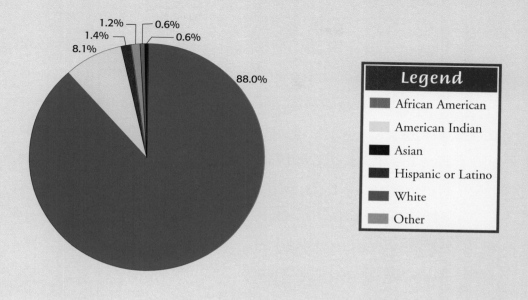

1.2%
1.4%
8.1%
0.6%
0.6%
88.0%

Legend
- African American
- American Indian
- Asian
- Hispanic or Latino
- White
- Other

In 1931, Ted and Dorothy Hustead bought a drug store in the small town of Wall, South Dakota. For nearly five years during the Great Depression, the store had very little business.

In the hot, dry summer of 1936, the Husteads had an idea. The highway that went by Wall was busy with travelers going to the Black Hills. The Husteads decided to offer free ice water to people traveling through Wall. They hoped this offer would draw the people into their store.

The Husteads made some signs to place on the highway. They spread their message over several signs. The signs were spaced apart so people could read them from the highway. The first series of signs said, "Get a soda . . . Get a root beer . . . turn next corner . . . Just as near . . . To Highway 16 & 14. . . Free Ice Water. . . Wall Drug." People began stopping at the Hustead's store right away to get free ice water. The Husteads were busy handing out free water, giving people directions, and selling ice cream cones.

The Wall Drug store has been a busy place ever since. The store now takes up an entire city block and includes a restaurant, gift shop, and museum. People stop to buy souvenirs and eat. They still get free ice water.

The Sturgis Rally is one of the largest motorcycle rallies in the country. The week-long event takes place every August. People attend the rally to be with others who share an interest in motorcycles. People buy equipment, look at each other's bikes, and have a good time. Many bikers compete in a

Today, Wall Drug store is owned and managed by Ted and Dorothy Hustead's son and grandsons.

Bikers filled Main Street during the Sturgis Motorcycle Rally in 2000.

motorcycle race. So many people attend the rally, the small town is completely overrun by motorcycle enthusiasts during the week. Some residents rent out their houses for the week. Others allow bikers to camp out on their lawns.

The world's only Corn Palace in Mitchell honors South Dakota's agriculture. Originally called the Corn Belt Exposition, the Corn Palace was started in 1892. It was a place for farmers to display their harvests. They placed their grains, corn, and wheat on the outside of the building.

The present building was completed in 1921. It serves as a place for sporting events and concerts. New murals are created each year with fresh grains, corn, straw, and wheat. The murals show typical South Dakota scenes, such as farms, pheasants, bison, and American Indian images.

Arts in South Dakota

Music, theater, art, and literature are important to South Dakota's culture. The South Dakota Symphony Orchestra performs concerts in Sioux Falls. A string quartet and a woodwind quintet of players from the symphony tour the state. They play at schools and teach students about music.

In Spearfish, the Black Hills Passion Play is an annual summer performance. This play tells about the last seven days of the life of Jesus Christ. Performances take place in an outdoor theater that is more than two city blocks long.

American Indians have also contributed to the arts in South Dakota. One of the state's most famous artists is Oscar Howe (1915–1983), a Yanktonai Sioux. He was born on the Crow Creek reservation in 1915. Howe is known for his abstract style of geometrical and swirling shapes. His paintings reflect Sioux tradition and culture.

Laura Ingalls Wilder (1867–1957) wrote a series of children's books about her life growing up in the 1870s and 1880s. Her books *By the Shores of Silver Lake* and *Little Town on the Prairie* are set in DeSmet, South Dakota. People visit the places where Laura and her family once lived.

The Land of Infinite Variety

From the state's many Indian reservations to tourist attractions like Wall Drug, South Dakota is truly a state of variety. The land changes from rolling farmland to rugged badlands to tree-covered Black Hills. With all this variety, South Dakota remains a laid-back and friendly place to live, work, and visit.

Artist Oscar Howe taught art classes at the University of South Dakota in Vermillion from 1957 to 1980.

Sunflower Seed Cookies

South Dakota ranks second in the country in sunflower seed production. The nut is the soft part of the sunflower seed inside the shell.

Ingredients

1½ cups (360 mL) white sugar
1½ cups (360 mL) butter or
    margarine
2 eggs
3 cups (720 mL) flour
1 tablespoon (15 mL) baking
    soda
1 tablespoon (15 mL) baking
    powder
1 cup (240 mL) sunflower nuts
1 teaspoon (5 mL) vanilla

Equipment

large mixing bowl
dry-ingredient measuring cups
electric mixer
small mixing bowl
measuring spoons
spoon
baking sheets
oven mitts
spatula
cooling rack

What You Do

1. Preheat oven to 350°F (180°C).

2. In a large bowl, cream together sugar, butter, and eggs with mixer.

3. Measure the flour, baking soda, and baking powder into a small mixing bowl.

4. Add the flour mixture to the sugar and butter mixture a little at a time, mixing as you go.

5. Stir in the sunflower seeds.

6. Scoop out spoonfuls of the dough and form 1-inch (2.5-centimeter) balls. Place the dough balls on an ungreased baking sheet about 2 inches (5 centimeters) apart.

7. Bake for 15 minutes or until the cookies are golden brown.

8. Wearing oven mitts, carefully remove baking sheet from oven. Allow cookies to cool on the baking sheet for 2 minutes.

9. With a spatula, place cookies on cooling rack to cool completely.

Makes about 6 dozen cookies

South Dakota's Flag and Seal

South Dakota's Flag

The South Dakota state flag is blue and features the state seal surrounded by a golden sun. The state name and its official nickname circle the seal. The current flag was adopted in 1992. That year, the nickname changed from the Sunshine State to the Mount Rushmore State.

South Dakota's State Seal

The state seal represents life in South Dakota. An image of the Missouri River flows through the middle of the seal. The dark mountains in the background represent the Black Hills. A farmer plowing a field shows that farming is important in South Dakota. Cattle represent the ranching industry. A mill and furnace on the left side of the river stand for manufacturing. The date 1889 is the year of statehood.

Almanac

General Facts

Nickname: Mount Rushmore State

Population: 754,844 (U.S. Census 2000)

Population rank: 46th

Capital: Pierre

Largest cities: Sioux Falls, Rapid City, Aberdeen, Watertown, Brookings

Agriculture

Agricultural products: Corn, soybeans, wheat, sunflower seeds, cattle, hogs, sheep

Climate

Average summer temperature: 70 degrees Fahrenheit (21 degrees Celsius)

Average winter temperature: 19 degrees Fahrenheit (minus 7 degrees Celsius)

Average annual precipitation: 18.3 inches (46.5 centimeters)

Geography

Area: 77,121 square miles (199,743 square kilometers)

Size rank: 17th largest

Highest point: Harney Peak, 7,242 feet (2,207 meters) above sea level

Lowest point: Big Stone Lake, 962 feet (293 meters) above sea level

American pasqueflower

Coyote

Symbols

Animal: Coyote

Bird: Chinese ring-necked pheasant

Dessert: Kuchen

Drink: Milk

Fish: Walleye

Flower: American pasqueflower

Economy

Natural resources: Fertile soil, gold, timber

Types of industry: Financial services, computer parts, food processing, tourism, health care

Symbols

Fossil: Triceratops

Insect: Honeybee

Jewelry: Black Hills gold

Song: "Hail, South Dakota," by Deecort Hammitt

Sport: Rodeo

Tree: Black Hills spruce

Government

First governor: Arthur Mellette, 1889–1893

Statehood: November 2, 1889; 40th state

U.S. Representatives: 1

U.S. Senators: 2

U.S. electoral votes: 3

Counties: 66

Timeline

State History

1600s
Sioux Indians are living in South Dakota.

1743
Louis-Joseph and Francois La Verendrye become the first European explorers to see South Dakota.

1804
Lewis and Clark explore the Missouri River in South Dakota.

1877
The Sioux Treaty gives the Black Hills to the United States.

1861
Dakota Territory is established.

U.S. History

1620
The Pilgrims establish a colony in North America.

1775–1783
American colonists fight for their independence from Great Britain in the Revolutionary War.

1812–1814
The United States and Great Britain fight the War of 1812.

1861–1865
The Civil War is fought between Northern and Southern states.

1889
South Dakota becomes the 40th state on November 2.

1927
Work begins on Mount Rushmore monument.

1980
U.S. Supreme Court rules that the U.S. government must pay the Sioux $106 million for the Black Hills; the Sioux refuse the money.

1996
Governor Bill Janklow starts a program to bring technology and Internet access to all schools in the state.

1890
Hundreds of Sioux are killed at Wounded Knee.

1973
Members of the American Indian Movement and other Indians take over Wounded Knee village.

1929–1939
The U.S. economy suffers during the Great Depression.

1964
The U.S. Congress passes the Civil Rights Act, which makes discrimination illegal.

1939–1945
World War II is fought; the United States enters the war in 1941.

2001
On September 11, terrorists attack the World Trade Center and the Pentagon.

1914–1918
World War I is fought; the United States enters the war in 1917.

Words to Know

butte (BYOOT)—a rocky mountain with steep sides and a flat top

immigrant (IM-uh-gruhnt)—a person who leaves one country to live in another country

initiative (i-NI-shuh-tiv)—a way for citizens to propose new state laws

interest (IN-tur-ist)—a fee paid for borrowing money; credit card companies charge interest.

mural (MYU-ruhl)—a work of art on a wall

reconciliation (rek-uhn-sil-ee-AY-shuhn)—the act of becoming friendly after a fight or disagreement

referendum (ref-uh-REN-duhm)—a public vote on a law passed by the legislature

reservation (rez-er-VAY-shun)—land owned and controlled by American Indians

soybean (SOI-been)—a seed that grows in pods on bushy plants; people use soybeans to make vegetable oil.

To Learn More

Hirschmann, Kris. *South Dakota, the Mount Rushmore State.* World Almanac Library of the States. Milwaukee: World Almanac Library, 2003.

Presnall, Judith Janda. *Mount Rushmore.* Building History Series. San Diego: Lucent Books, 2000.

Todd, Anne M. *Crazy Horse, 1842–1877.* American Indian Biographies. Mankato, Minn.: Blue Earth Books, 2003.

Waldman, Neil. *Wounded Knee.* New York: Atheneum Books for Young Readers, 2001.

Walsh Shepherd, Donna. *South Dakota.* America the Beautiful. New York: Children's Press, 2001.

Internet Sites

Do you want to find out more about South Dakota?
Let FactHound, our fact-finding hound dog, do the research for you.

Here's how:
1) Visit ***http://www.facthound.com***
2) Type in the **Book ID number:**
   0736821988
3) Click on **FETCH IT**.

FactHound will fetch Internet sites picked by our editors just for you!

Places to Write and Visit

Center for Western Studies
2201 S. Summit Avenue, Box 727
Augustana College
Sioux Falls, SD 57197

Corn Palace
601 North Main
Mitchell, SD 57301

Crazy Horse Memorial
Avenue of the Chiefs
Crazy Horse, SD 57730

Cultural Heritage Center
900 Governors Drive
Pierre, SD 57501

Governor's Office
500 East Capitol Street
Pierre, SD 57501

Mount Rushmore National Memorial
Highway 244, P.O. Box 268
Keystone, SD 57751-0268

Wall Drug Store
510 Main Street
Wall, SD 57790

The face of Crazy Horse was completed in 1998. The face is nine stories high. The white outline shows where the horse's head will be.

Index

West Union School
23870 NW West Union Road
Hillsboro, Oregon 97124